FROZEN IN THE PAST
The Cost of Holding Back

by Rebecca Obeng

ABOUT THE BOOK

FROZEN IN THE PAST: The Cost of Holding Back is a powerful and reflective journey through the stories of biblical women who struggled to let go of pain, pride, people, and the past. From Lot's wife who looked back, to Herodias's daughter who danced for someone else's bitterness, each chapter unearths emotional truths that still shape modern lives today.

This book is not just about them, it's about us. The ones who stay stuck in familiar pain. The ones who confuse silence with strength. The ones who carry wounds that were never meant to define us. And yet, within each story is a mirror and an invitation.

Through rich biblical insight, modern-day parallels, emotional depth, and soul-searching reflection, Frozen in the Past exposes what happens when we refuse to release what God is calling us to let go of. But it doesn't stop there. The book also offers redemptive portraits of women who did let go, and found healing, purpose, and restoration on the other side.

This is a book for:

The woman still grieving what could've been

The daughter who inherited emotional battles not her own

The woman clinging to control because surrender feels too risky

Anyone tired of surviving, performing, or pretending

Every soul longing for the courage to finally let go

You don't have to stay frozen.

You can become the woman who reached.

You can become the woman who let go.

And you can walk into a future unbound by the past.

Copyright © 2025 by Rebecca Obeng

All rights reserved.

No part of this publication may be reproduced, stored in a retrieval system, or transmitted in any form or by any means, electronic, mechanical, photocopy, recording, or otherwise, without the prior written permission of the author, except in the case of brief quotations used in reviews, articles, or other non-commercial uses permitted by copyright law.

ISBN: 978-1-7640905-2-0

This book offers testimony, biblical instruction, and spiritual guidance, created to inspire and support individuals seeking healing and deliverance through Christ.

Table of Contents

ENDORSEMENT 7

PREFACE 9

INTRODUCTION 10

CHAPTER 1 12

    Lot's Wife, When the Past Feels Safer than the Promise 12

CHAPTER 2 21

    Dinah — When Silence Screams and Closure Never Comes 21

CHAPTER 3 37

    Naomi -When Bitterness Becomes a Home 37

CHAPTER 4 47

    Michal — Loving What No Longer Exists 47

CHAPTER 5 60

    Orpah — The Goodbye That Didn't Birth a Legacy .. 60

CHAPTER 6 67

    The Woman at the Well — Cycles That Never Let Go of You 67

CHAPTER 7 83

    Sapphira — When Letting Go Means Letting Go of Control 83

CHAPTER 8 90

    Herodias's Daughter — When Vengeance Becomes Your Vision 90

CONCLUSION 103

    The Woman Who Let Go 103

EPILOGUE	117
A Letter to the Woman Becoming Free	117
GLOSSARY	121
Alabaster Jar	121
ACKNOWLEDGMENTS	125
READER NOTES	127
Open Lined Notes Page	129

ENDORSEMENT

If you're looking for a book that will inspire, challenge, and empower you, [FROZEN IN THE PAST] is incredible. I found it incredibly helpful, and I believe you will, too. This book provides a fresh perspective on [Frozen in place, forever stuck between destruction and destiny.] and is an essential resource for anyone seeking to understand [to move in life, live again as a believer in Christ Jesus]. Highly recommended."

From Maxwell's Note: Australia

Rebecca Obeng has crafted a spiritually potent and emotionally resonant work that speaks to the silent burdens many women carry. Frozen in the Past is a compelling blend of biblical reflection and therapeutic insight, offering healing and clarity for women navigating the emotional toll of holding on to pain, people, and patterns that God may be calling them to release.

Frozen in the Past is a timely, transformative, and tender guide for every woman navigating the pain of her past while longing for freedom in her future. Rebecca Obeng has not only written a book—she has opened a door for healing. With literary elegance and spiritual precision, she invites the reader to rise, release, and reclaim. This work stands as both a mirror and a map—a mirror of the soul's hidden wounds and a map toward restoration.

Highly recommended for women's ministries, personal healing journeys, and anyone seeking faith-filled emotional renewal.

By Martin Ejenobo: Nigeria

Rebecca offers a strength-based, heart-warming, and Spirit-led journey of reflection, inviting women to prayerfully believe, confront, and rise above the emotional, spiritual, and relational obstacles that hinder personal growth and freedom, keeping them tethered to past experiences. Through insightful narratives grounded in the lived experiences of biblical women, she presents Christ-cantered case studies that serve as mirrors and guides toward healing, surrender, and transformation. Emphasizing the importance of releasing pain, pride, and the illusion of control, _Frozen in the Past_ calls readers to embrace the freedom, divine purpose, and bold faith that come from trusting God and stepping into the future He has lovingly prepared, unshackled by the past and anchored in His grace.

Apostle Eric Emanuel Marfo Sekyere Australia

PREFACE

There are moments in life when we know it's time to move on, yet something in us clings tightly to what once was. I've seen it in the mirror. I've seen it in the stories of women who are still trying to salvage broken relationships, waiting for closure that may never come, or grieving old versions of themselves.

This book was born out of a personal journey. I've wrestled with goodbyes I didn't want to say. I've tried to resurrect things God was clearly putting to rest. And somewhere along the way, I met Lot's wife not just in scripture, but in spirit. She looked back, and so have I. Maybe you have, too.

This is not a book about judgment. It is a book about understanding why we freeze emotionally, spiritually, and mentally when we're called to move forward. It is about women who got stuck. It's about you and me. It's about grace. It's about release.

I pray that as you read, you find pieces of your own journey in these pages. May this book be the nudge, the mirror, and the invitation you need to finally let go and never look back.

Rebecca Obeng

INTRODUCTION

She doesn't even have a name. In one of the Bible's most dramatic moments of divine judgment and deliverance, a woman becomes a monument not of faith or heroism, but of hesitation. Lot's wife looked back. And she became a pillar of salt. Frozen in place, forever stuck between destruction and destiny.

Her story is barely a verse, yet it speaks volumes. She was fleeing a city God had condemned. She had the chance to start over. But something pulled her gaze and perhaps her heart back. And in that split second, everything changed. How many of us have stood at that same threshold? We start to walk away from something toxic, but the comfort of familiarity calls us back. We leave a season God told us to exit, but we keep replaying the "what ifs." We receive healing, but still wear the identity of the wounded. We're offered purpose, but refuse to let go of people or places that no longer serve it. This book is not just about Lot's wife. It is about every woman who has struggled to leave the past behind, who has been emotionally or spiritually immobilised by regret, attachment, trauma, or comfort. Looking back isn't always physical, it's internal, it's living in yesterday when God has already opened the door to tomorrow.

Through the stories of several biblical women, and the wisdom their lives offer, we'll uncover what it truly costs to hold back when God is calling us forward. And more importantly, how to break free from that grip.

Let this be your invitation to thaw. To move. To heal. To live again.

CHAPTER 1

Lot's Wife, When the Past Feels Safer than the Promise

Scripture Focus:

"But Lot's wife looked back, and she became a pillar of salt."

Genesis 19:26 (NIV)

The Silent Turn

She doesn't speak. She doesn't cry out.

There is no recorded plea, no argument, no explanation, just a turn.

A backward glance that cost her everything.

Why did she look back?

Was it fear, mourning, curiosity, or a moment of disbelief? Lot's wife had been given a clear instruction: Don't look back. But obedience is hard when your heart is still tied to what you're leaving behind. Perhaps she wasn't just leaving a city, she was leaving her identity, her memories, her comforts, her friends. Maybe her other children were still in Sodom. Maybe she loved the life she had built there. Whatever the case, the past called her name louder than her future did. And it turned her into a monument of warning: be careful what you hold onto.

The Safety of the Familiar

So often, we romanticise the past because it's familiar. Even if it was painful, at least we understood it. At least we knew how to survive in it. But deliverance isn't about survival, it's about freedom. Lot's wife wasn't punished because she felt loss. She was immobilised because she let her longing override her obedience. And how often do we do the same? We know the relationship is unhealthy, but it's familiar. We know God is calling us to change, but comfort feels easier. We know our worth, but fear convinces us to settle again.

So we pause, we linger, we turn. Familiarity feels like safety, not because it's good, but because it's predictable. And predictability gives the illusion of control. Lot's wife wasn't just leaving a city. She was leaving her rhythm, her comfort zone, her identity. Perhaps she was even leaving family, children, friends, memories she wasn't ready to surrender. The streets of Sodom may have been corrupt, but they were home. And sometimes, the comfort of what we know outweighs the promise of what we can't yet see. Familiarity can be a prison with velvet bars. We don't realise how tightly we're holding on until God asks us to let go.

We see this everywhere: Women stay in relationships that break them because the fear of being alone feels more threatening than the pain they already know. People remain in unfulfilling jobs because they've built their entire identity around what they do, not who they are. Some of us cling to guilt or shame because we've worn them so long, they feel like truth. Others hold onto bitterness, believing that if they let it go, justice might never come. There's a strange contradiction in transformation: healing often feels like grieving. The moment we are called to move forward, we also face the loss of who we used to be. And sometimes, that loss is what we fear the most. The healed version of ourselves feels risky. Vulnerable. Unfamiliar. But the broken version? That one we understand. That one, we know how to survive.

"She knew he wasn't good for her. The lies, the emotional distance, and the silent punishments she had cried over them a hundred times. But she stayed. Because leaving meant rewriting everything, and she didn't know who she'd be without him. So she stayed. And with every year that passed, she disappeared a little more." Sometimes we grieve what God has already judged. Sometimes we hold on to what God has already let go of. And in doing so, we stunt our own deliverance. Lot's wife didn't just disobey a command; she doubted the goodness of what was ahead. Her backward glance was more than a moment of weakness. It was a declaration: I'm not sure I trust what God is offering more than what I'm leaving.

And we've all done it in some way.

Looking back isn't just about nostalgia. It's often a crisis of faith.

Do you trust that what's ahead is worth the uncertainty?

Do you trust that who you're becoming is more valuable than who you used to be?

Do you trust that God isn't leading you into a void, but into victory?

Freedom often looks like fear at first glance. But the promise is not behind you, it's ahead.

Modern-Day Pillars of Salt

Some of us aren't physically stuck, but emotionally we are frozen.

We replay conversations.

We hold onto old identities.

We live with resentment or nostalgia so strong that it keeps us from walking in purpose.

Looking back can cost you your future.

What are you looking back at?

What still holds your gaze?

Lot's wife was turned into a literal pillar of salt, but many of us are living as emotional or spiritual pillars of salt. Not because we turned our heads physically, but because we turned our hearts inward. We froze in moments that were meant to be passed through. We paused when God told us to move.

You may not see it in the mirror, but you feel it:

Stuck in cycles you can't seem to break, paralysed by decisions you should have made long ago.

Numb in places where joy or hope used to live, craving change, yet afraid of the cost it demands.

You can look alive but be spiritually motionless, you show up, you smile, you function. But somewhere deep inside, you've stopped moving. The trauma, the disappointment, the betrayal, the regret it arrested your movement. And like Lot's wife, you were caught between what God was destroying and what He was trying to deliver you into. Sometimes, you don't even realise you've become a pillar. You've simply grown accustomed to standing still. You no longer dream, risk, trust, or pursue. You're just there, frozen in a moment, a memory, or a mindset.

What Does Being a Pillar Look Like Today?

- Staying emotionally connected to someone God has already removed from your life.

You replay conversations, scroll through their social media, fantasise about reconciliation, even though everything in your spirit says: Let it go.

- Identifying yourself by your lowest moment.

You don't see yourself as redeemed or restored. You still live in the shadow of your failure, your past, your shame.

- Carrying unforgiveness like armour.

You think it protects you, but in truth, it hardens you. You haven't moved on, you've just grown cold.

Romanticising the past because the future feels too uncertain. You remember Sodom without remembering the fire. You think back on the relationship, the career, the version of yourself from "back then" and wonder, Was it really so bad? You start justifying bondage because freedom feels frightening.

The Subtlety of Being Stuck

Some pillars of salt walk among us in church pews and corporate offices. They raise families. They post scriptures. They check the boxes of life, but inside? They stopped hoping, stopped believing, stopped healing.

They are existing, not becoming.

They are the ones who say:

"I'm fine" with a smile that never reaches their eyes.

"I don't need anyone" because trusting again feels impossible.

"Maybe this is just my lot in life" because dreaming again feels dangerous.

"That's just who I am now", because they've surrendered to the freeze.

But Here's the Hope

You don't have to stay a pillar.

You can thaw. You can walk again.

You can let the past be what it was, and no longer let it define who you are.

The pain may be real. The memories may still sting. But they are not meant to hold you captive. They are part of your story, not the end of it.

God is still calling you forward.

He hasn't stopped speaking just because you stopped moving.

You don't have to stay stuck in that moment. You don't have to keep living in the freeze.

Reflection Questions

Is there something God has clearly asked you to let go of, but you keep returning to in your thoughts or emotions?

What emotions surface when you think about releasing the past, fear, grief, guilt, uncertainty?

How has holding back affected your spiritual, emotional, or relational growth?

Prayer of Release

Lord,

I confess that I have been looking back.

Back at what hurt, what felt safe, what I hoped would work.

Today, I choose to trust your direction more than my emotions.

Unfreeze my heart. Help me to move forward, even when I don't have all the answers.

Teach me to let go and let you write the next chapter of my life.

Amen.

Letting Go Moment

Write down one thing you know God is asking you to release.

It could be a memory, a person, a fear, or a dream that no longer serves His purpose.

Then write this over it in bold:

"I am not going back. I am moving forward."

CHAPTER 2

Dinah — When Silence Screams and Closure Never Comes

Scripture Focus:

"Now Dinah, the daughter Leah had borne to Jacob, went out to visit the women of the land."

Genesis 34:1 (NIV)

The Unspoken Wound

Her story begins with a visit, and ends with silence.

Dinah, the only named daughter of Jacob, ventured out to see the women of the land. What seemed like a simple visit quickly descended into trauma. She was violated by Shechem, the son of a local ruler. The text does not record her voice. Not once. She is a character in her own story, but without a say. And that silence? It echoes across centuries. It mirrors the experience of countless women whose pain goes unnamed, unheard, or unresolved. Dinah became a casualty not only of violence but of being swallowed by the silence that followed.

When Closure Never Comes

We often assume healing follows pain, that time always offers resolution. But what about the times it doesn't? What happens when the wound stays open? When your name is in the story, but your voice is not?

Dinah's trauma was followed by rage, not hers, but her brothers'. Their response was violent, bloody, and ultimately costly for their family. Still, Dinah's own healing? Never discussed. Her future? Unknown. Her story ends not with justice or redemption, but with being taken out of the house, as if to say, "She needs to be removed from view." Sometimes, we're not frozen because we're looking back. We're frozen because we never had the chance to speak. Because our story was never allowed to breathe.

We are taught, sometimes subtly, sometimes directly, that pain should have a neat ending. That wounds should heal cleanly with time. That people will eventually apologise, that justice will prevail, and that the hurt will make sense one day. But real life doesn't always work that way.

For Dinah, there was no justice rendered for her. No community-wide lament. No recorded comfort. Her story is sandwiched between political deals, family vengeance, and a deafening silence. The reader is left wondering what became of her, but more heartbreakingly, did anyone care enough to ask? Closure is often described as a final chapter, a wrapping-up of loose ends. But what happens when the story just… stops?

The Pain of Unfinished Stories

What happens when the person who hurt you never says sorry?

When the trauma doesn't have a reason, or the reason doesn't satisfy?

When the apology comes too late, or not at all?

When the damage done is permanent, and the perpetrator moves on as if nothing happened?

This is where many women live, in the unfinished chapters.

Waiting for the call that never comes.

Hoping for the truth that remains hidden.

Looking for a reason that explains the suffering.

Trying to tie together the frayed edges of pain that refuses to be clean.

Some of us don't need justice, we just want acknowledgment.

We want someone to say, "That should not have happened to you."

We want someone to sit in our pain without trying to fix it.

We want someone to say the words that were missing: "I believe you."

"You didn't deserve that."

"You matter."

Letting Go Without Answers

The hardest healing is the kind that requires surrendering the need for clarity. It's one thing to heal with a full picture, it's another to heal when the picture was stolen. Sometimes, closure doesn't come from the person or situation, it has to come from God. And sometimes, even God won't explain everything. He'll just offer presence. He'll offer healing. He'll offer peace that passes understanding, even when there's no understanding at all. That's where faith becomes deeply personal. Not just believing in God, but believing that your healing is still valid, even if you never get what you think you need.

Modern Reflections of Dinah

A daughter waits for her father to return and explain why he left. He never does.

A woman tries to ask her ex why he ghosted her after five years of emotional investment. His silence screams louder than words.

A childhood abuse survivor finally finds the courage to speak, only to be met with disbelief or deflection.

A woman carries the weight of being overlooked, dismissed, misunderstood, and no one even knows what she's had to survive quietly. These women become experts at performing okay-ness.

They excel. They lead. They serve. But deep down, there is a still-open wound that whispers: You never got to say goodbye. You never got to be heard.

The Weight of the Unsaid

So many women live in that space between experience and expression. They carry memories too heavy to name, experiences that altered them but were dismissed or silenced.

You don't have to be a victim of assault to understand Dinah's reality. Her story resonates with anyone who:

Was told to "get over it" before they even knew how to process it.

Was never given the language to grieve what happened.

Felt invisible in their own pain.

Watched others take over their narrative while they stood on the sidelines of their own healing.

Dinah reminds us: Silence can freeze you in place just as powerfully as nostalgia.

The Weight of the Unsaid, this is the kind of pain that doesn't scream. It doesn't shout for attention. It simply lingers, quiet, heavy, and unresolved.

Dinah's story is wrapped in that kind of silence. She is introduced. She is violated. And then she disappears. Not a single word from her lips is recorded. Not a cry. Not a lament. Not a plea for justice. She becomes a character whose trauma shapes the actions of others, while her own healing or even her presence is erased from the narrative.

Her voice was taken before it was even given space.

And that is the weight of the unsaid:

It's the grief that has no outlet.

The rage that has no release.

The confusion that has no clarity.

The injustice that has no closure.

It's when something life-altering happens to you, but no one asks how you feel.

It's when the world moves on, but you're still stuck in the moment.

It's when your story is rewritten by others, and you're left wondering if your version will ever matter.

The Burden of Silence: Real Stories of the Unspoken

Leila's Story

Leila was 16 when her uncle made an inappropriate comment that led to years of subtle grooming. When she finally told her mother, the response was dismissive: "He's family. Don't blow this out of proportion."

So Leila never spoke about it again. She grew up believing her pain was an inconvenience. Now in her 30s, she still finds herself shrinking in rooms, unable to advocate for herself in relationships or work, because somewhere deep inside, her voice still feels unwelcome.

Tasha's Story

Tasha had a miscarriage during her second trimester. Friends didn't know how to comfort her, so they said things like, "At least you weren't further along" or "You can try again." Her pain was spiritual, emotional, physical and invisible. At church, she felt pressure to "praise through it." But inside, she was grieving deeply. She never cried in front of anyone. Now, five years later, she still wonders who that child might have been, but she's never spoken about it out loud.

Janet's Story

Janet is a strong friend. The one who checks in on everyone, offers advice, and keeps going no matter what. What her friends don't know is that her strength comes from survival. She was emotionally neglected as a child. Every time she felt pain, she was told to be grateful and stop complaining. So now, even in adult friendships, she hides her needs, fears, and emotions. She doesn't know how to ask for help. Not because she doesn't want to, but because she was never taught that she could.

Invisible but Impactful

The danger of unvoiced pain is that it becomes identity-shaping.

When no one acknowledges what happened, we start to believe it wasn't worth acknowledging.

When no one validates our hurt, we begin to wonder if we were the problem.

And slowly, we stop expecting space. We stop asking for understanding.

We carry on, but not as whole people.

We perform strength while privately unravelling.

Unspoken pain doesn't disappear. It compounds.

It leaks into how we show up.

It influences who we trust.

It shapes what we expect from love, faith, and ourselves.

Your Voice Was Never Meant to Be Buried

Dinah's story is the story of every woman who has been left without closure, resolution, or recognition. It's the story of every woman who has had to move forward while carrying what no one was willing to hold with her.

But here's the truth:

God saw Dinah. And He sees you.

You were never invisible to Him. You were never voiceless in His presence.

And He invites you now, not to shout, but to whisper if you must.

To say what you've never said. To name what has never been named.

Because the weight of the unsaid begins to lift the moment you speak.

And you don't have to be loud to be heard by heaven.

Breaking the Freeze

Maybe your trauma was loud. Maybe it was quiet.

But either way, it deserves attention. Healing. A voice.

What keeps us frozen isn't always the inability to move, it's the inability to be heard.

If no one acknowledges the pain, how can you release it?

Dinah's story is a wake-up call: We must speak. Even if it trembles.

We must feel. Even if it's messy.

We must grieve. Even if the world tells us to move on.

Your story matters. It matters even if it's unfinished.

You don't need closure to begin healing.

The Invitation of Unfinished Healing

God doesn't require that your story be tidy before He begins to restore you.

You can be half-healed, half-hopeful, half-believing, and He will still meet you there.

You can still be waiting for answers, and He will begin to write a new story from the place where the old one broke. Closure, in the Kingdom of God, doesn't always look like a perfect ending.

Sometimes it looks like peace in the middle of questions.

Sometimes it's choosing to breathe again, to walk again, and to live again, even if you never get an apology.

> *"Closure isn't always a conversation, it's a decision. A sacred surrender to live even when the past didn't end the way it should have."*

Reflection Questions

Have you ever felt like your story wasn't fully told, or that your voice was ignored?

Are there parts of your pain that you've never allowed yourself to process out loud?

What would it mean for you to give voice to your silence today?

Prayer for the Silenced

Lord,

You see what others missed. You hear what was never spoken.

Today, I bring my silent places to you.

The wounds I buried. The words I swallowed. The moments I never named.

Help me find my voice again.

Give me the courage to speak, to feel, and to heal.

I will no longer be defined by silence.

Amen.

Letting Go Moment

Take a piece of paper. Write a letter to the version of yourself that went through "that moment."

Tell her everything you wish someone had said.

Tell her she is not to blame.

Then, write this at the bottom of the page:

"My silence ends here. My healing begins now."

Isaiah 60 : 1- 22

The Glory of Zion (You)
60 "Arise, shine, for your light has come,
and the glory of the Lord rises upon you.
2 See, darkness covers the earth
and thick darkness is over the peoples,
but the Lord rises upon you
and his glory appears over you.
3 Nations will come to your light,
and kings to the brightness of your dawn.
4 "Lift up your eyes and look about you:
All assemble and come to you;
your sons come from afar,
and your daughters are carried on the hip.
5 Then you will look and be radiant,

your heart will throb and swell with joy;
the wealth on the seas will be brought to you,
to you the riches of the nations will come.
6 Herds of camels will cover your land,
young camels of Midian and Ephah.
And all from Sheba will come,
bearing gold and incense
and proclaiming the praise of the Lord.
7 All Kedar's flocks will be gathered to you,
the rams of Nebaioth will serve you;
they will be accepted as offerings on my altar,
and I will adorn my glorious temple.
8 "Who are these that fly along like clouds,
like doves to their nests?
9 Surely the islands look to me;
in the lead are the ships of Tarshish,[a]
bringing your children from afar,
with their silver and gold,
to the honour of the Lord your God,
the Holy One of Israel,
for he has endowed you with splendour.
10 "Foreigners will rebuild your walls,
and their kings will serve you.
Though in anger I struck you,
in favour I will show you compassion.

11 Your gates will always stand open,
they will never be shut, day or night,
so that people may bring you the wealth of the nations,
their kings led in triumphal procession.
12 For the nation or kingdom that will not serve you will perish;
it will be utterly ruined.
13 "The glory of Lebanon will come to you,
the juniper, the fir and the cypress together,
to adorn my sanctuary;
and I will glorify the place for my feet.
14 The children of your oppressors will come bowing before you;
all who despise you will bow down at your feet
and will call you the City of the Lord,
Zion of the Holy One of Israel.
15 "Although you have been forsaken and hated,
with no one traveling through,
I will make you the everlasting pride
and the joy of all generations.
16 You will drink the milk of nations
and be nursed at royal breasts.
Then you will know that I, the Lord, am your Savior,
your Redeemer, the Mighty One of Jacob.
17 Instead of bronze I will bring you gold,
and silver in place of iron.
Instead of wood I will bring you bronze,

and iron in place of stones.
I will make peace your governor
and well-being your ruler.
18 No longer will violence be heard in your land,
nor ruin or destruction within your borders,
but you will call your walls Salvation
and your gates Praise.
19 The sun will no more be your light by day,
nor will the brightness of the moon shine on you,
for the Lord will be your everlasting light,
and your God will be your glory.
20 Your sun will never set again,
and your moon will wane no more;
the Lord will be your everlasting light,
and your days of sorrow will end.
21 Then all your people will be righteous
and they will possess the land forever.
They are the shoot I have planted,
the work of my hands,
for the display of my splendour.
22 The least of you will become a thousand,
the smallest a mighty nation.
I am the Lord;
in its time I will do this swiftly.

CHAPTER 3

Naomi - When Bitterness Becomes a Home

Scripture Focus:

"Don't call me Naomi," she told them. "Call me Mara, because the Almighty has made my life very bitter."

Ruth 1:20 (NIV)

The Woman Who Renamed Herself

When Naomi returned to Bethlehem after years in Moab, the women barely recognised her. She left full. She came back empty. Her husband was gone. Her sons were buried. Her heart was fractured.

She didn't just return physically changed, she returned emotionally renamed.

"Don't call me Naomi," she said, which means "pleasant."

"Call me Mara," she insisted, which means "bitter."

Bitterness had become her identity.

Naomi wasn't just mourning her loss; she was living in it. She moved in, unpacked, and made her home in grief. And sometimes, when life breaks us repeatedly, bitterness doesn't knock, it settles in quietly. Like a shadow. Like an unwelcome guest that becomes a permanent resident in the heart.

The Slow Fade into Bitterness

Bitterness doesn't always start loud. Sometimes it starts as disappointment. A hope deferred. A dream that keeps slipping away. A prayer that goes unanswered. A betrayal that wounds deeper than anyone knows.

Over time, the pain calcifies. And without release, it becomes:

Cynicism.

Numbness.

Emotional detachment.

Harshness toward others who still have what you lost.

We don't always recognise it because bitterness doesn't always scream. Sometimes it speaks through sarcasm. Cold silence. Withdrawal. Or the inner vow that says, "I'll never let myself feel like that again."

Bitterness as a False Refuge that Traps You

Bitterness doesn't always feel destructive at first. Sometimes, it feels like protection.

When your heart has been shattered by loss, betrayal, disappointment, or unanswered prayers, bitterness offers a shell. A fortress. A place to hide your vulnerability so no one can wound you again.

It whispers things like:

"If you stop caring, you won't get hurt."

"If you expect the worst, you'll never be disappointed."

"If you harden your heart, you'll never be broken again."

And so we let it in. Not because we want to become bitter, but because it feels safer than staying soft. It promises security, but gives us solitude. It offers armour, but steals intimacy. It pretends to be strength, but breeds cynicism. Bitterness numbs us. It convinces us that feeling nothing is better than feeling broken again.

But numbness is not healing.

And surviving is not the same as living.

At first, bitterness feels like a strong tower.

But over time, it becomes a prison.

A place where joy cannot enter.

A place where even love feels suspicious.

A place where trust is foreign and tenderness feels like weakness.

You start seeing the world through a distorted lens:

People aren't kind, they're fake.

Opportunities aren't blessings, they're traps.

Compliments aren't genuine, they're manipulative.

God's silence isn't patience, it's punishment.

Bitterness builds walls where healing was meant to build bridges.

When You Let Bitterness Rename You

Naomi renamed herself, and many of us do the same.

"I'm just unlucky in love."

"People always leave."

"Nothing good ever lasts for me."

"I'm not one of the chosen ones."

"I should just accept that I'm meant to suffer."

We redefine our lives not by God's promises, but by our pain.

We let loss narrate our identity.

We start to believe that our story is over just because a chapter ended in devastation.

But here's the truth Naomi didn't see in that moment: God wasn't done with her yet.

Even in her bitterness, she was still on the path of redemption.

Even when she renamed herself, God never changed His plan.

Bitterness Feels Safer Than Hope

Hope is risky. It requires you to believe again.

To trust again.

To try again.

And when you've suffered deeply like Naomi, losing a husband, burying not one but two sons, hope feels dangerous. Reaching again feels foolish.

So bitterness says: "Don't reach." Just stay here. Be guarded. Be tough. Expect nothing. Feel nothing.

But the cost of this so-called safety is steep:

You stop celebrating others because their joy reminds you of your pain.

You stop praying earnestly because you're afraid to be let down again.

You stop seeing opportunities because you're too focused on what didn't work out before.

You stop believing that restoration is possible because you've confused survival with fulfilment.

Bitterness numbs us. It convinces us that feeling nothing is better than feeling broken again.

But numbness is not healing.

And surviving is not the same as living.

Ruth Was Right There

It's easy to forget that when Naomi renamed herself Mara, Ruth was standing beside her.

Ruth, the woman who refused to leave her.

Ruth, the very vessel through which God would restore Naomi's legacy.

Ruth, the beginning of Naomi's redemption, standing in her grief-blurred view.

Bitterness can blind us to the blessings we still have.

While Naomi mourned what was lost, she couldn't yet see what had been gained: loyalty, provision, legacy, a future. Sometimes we ask God for a miracle, and He sends us a Ruth. But if we're too bitter, we won't recognise her.

The Ruth You Can't See, Naomi was so swallowed by bitterness that she couldn't recognise the gift standing beside her: Ruth. Bitterness blinds us to our "Ruths", the blessings that still remain. The people who choose us even in our emptiness. The open doors we didn't expect. The quiet miracles are already unfolding. The gentle nudges of grace that bitterness makes us too calloused to feel. Bitterness doesn't just affect how you feel, it distorts what you see. And sometimes, we miss divine provision not because it isn't there, but because we're too wounded to trust it.

Modern Reflections of Naomi

A woman who gave her all to her family, only to be left behind, and now defines herself by what she sacrificed, not who she is.

A widow who believes her best years died with her spouse.

A mother who lost a child and now finds it difficult to smile without guilt.

A single woman who watched everyone else get married quietly built a home in disappointment.

A professional who was overlooked too many times and now believes she'll never be more than second-best.

Bitterness isn't just about anger. It's about unprocessed pain that has settled into identity.

But God Doesn't Call You Mara

God never addressed Naomi as "Mara."

He didn't affirm her new identity.

Why? Because our pain may rename us, but God never stops seeing us according to our purpose, not our pain. You may feel bitter. You may feel broken. But you are still called. Still chosen. Still held. Still seen. God didn't rename Naomi, He redeemed her.

A Soft Heart Is Still Possible

Bitterness is not the final chapter unless you let it be.

God invites us back into vulnerability, not to harm us, but to heal us.

He calls us back into softness, not for weakness, but for wholeness.

He calls us out of our self-made shelters, not to expose us, but to embrace us.

Naomi thought God had dealt bitterly with her.

But the same God who felt absent in Moab was the God who prepared a redeemer named Boaz.

A lineage that would lead to David.

A legacy that would one day birth the Messiah.

Bitterness was not the end. It was only a page.

And so it is for you.

Reflection Questions

Have you allowed a painful season to rename you?

What thoughts or internal vows has bitterness planted in your mind?

Who or what in your life might be a "Ruth" that you've been too hurt to recognise?

Prayer for the Bitter Heart

Lord,

I bring you the places I've stopped hoping.

The parts of me that have settled into sorrow.

The pieces of my identity that pain has tried to rewrite.

I confess that I've allowed bitterness to become my covering.

But today, I ask You to rename me, not according to my past, but Your promise.

Heal me. Restore me. Help me to hope again.

Amen.

Letting Go Moment

Write down the word or label that bitterness has tried to give you (e.g. forgotten, unlucky, unwanted, used, unworthy).

Then cross it out boldly and write this over it:

"God calls me Naomi, pleasant, whole, and restored. I will not live by the name pain gave me."

Isaiah 62: 4 APM

It will no longer be said of you [Judah], "Azubah (Abandoned)," Nor will it any longer be said of your land, "Shemamah (Desolate)"; But you will be called, "Hephzibah (My Delight is in Her)," And your land, "Married"; For the Lord delights in you, And to Him your land will be married [owned and protected by the Lord]

CHAPTER 4

Michal — Loving What No Longer Exists

Scripture Focus:

"Now Michal, Saul's daughter, loved David..."

1 Samuel 18:20 (NIV)

"But when she saw King David leaping and dancing before the Lord, she despised him in her heart."

2 Samuel 6:16 (NIV)

The Woman Who Fell in Love with a Rising Star

Michal loved David, she didn't just marry him, she chose him. He was young, brave, and admired. The giant slayer and the future king. Their love had the markings of romance and divine promise. But the story didn't unfold the way fairy tales do, soon after their union, chaos entered. Her father, Saul, turned on David. David fled, and Michal was left behind. Then she was given to another man and was then reclaimed by force, not by affection, when David rose to power. Let's look at this:

- What started as love became duty, that which once held passion now held political weight.

- And when David finally returned with victory and worship, Michal watched from a window and despised him in her heart.

When you're in Love with a Memory

Michal's story is the story of many of us women who fell in love with a version of someone or ourselves that no longer exists.

She remembered the David who once loved her.

Who once fought for her.

Who once made her feel seen.

But David was gone. Time, trauma, power, and distance had changed everything.

And she was still holding on to the idea of what used to be.

Many of us are like Michal. Still in love with the memory of a relationship, still grieving the person someone once was before they changed or left. Still attached to a dream that died years ago but feels too sacred to bury. We sit by the window of our lives, watching others dance into joy and freedom, while our hearts grow cold with silent disappointment. The danger of holding on too tightly. Love is powerful, but when it becomes an idol, it can turn toxic. Michal's love for David had once been pure, but when it wasn't reciprocated, when it wasn't honoured, when it wasn't returned, her love turned inward and hardened. Unreturned love can become resentment, and unprocessed pain can become pride. When we hold on to a version of someone that God is trying to release us from, we end up bitter, stagnant, and emotionally paralysed.

Frozen at the Window

Michal never joined David in his praise.

She didn't rejoice with the people.

She didn't celebrate the return of the Ark.

Instead, she remained at the window, disconnected from joy, removed from movement, isolated in judgment. How many of us are stuck at emotional windows? Watching others love freely, while we guard our hearts with sarcasm and suspicion. Seeing others heal and move forward, while we stay stuck in cycles of old pain. Observing life unfold, but unable to engage because our hearts are still tethered to what once was. The window becomes a metaphor for where we get stuck, on the edge of healing, but unwilling to enter.

The Pain Behind the Pride

It's easy to judge Michal's contempt.

But her pain was real.

She had been used, forgotten, and replaced.

She wasn't just bitter, she was broken.

Beneath her sarcasm was sorrow.

Beneath her judgment was grief.

Beneath her pride was a heart that once believed in love, and never healed when that love left.

- **Unpacking Michal's Emotional Walls**

At first glance, Michal's reaction to David's worship seems harsh, even arrogant. She mocks him from the window as he dances before the Lord, accuses him of shameless behaviour, and shows no joy at the Ark's return. But beneath her sharp words was a wounded heart.

Michal wasn't just bitter, but she was broken as well.

She had once loved David with all her heart. She protected him, even defying her own father to help him escape Saul's wrath. She risked everything for him. But in the years that followed, David moved forward, into war, into leadership, into other marriages.

Michal was left behind.

The pain of being unseen is one of the deepest wounds a heart can carry.

She wasn't just angry that David danced, she was devastated that he no longer looked at her the way he once did.

- **When Pride is a Defence Mechanism**

For many women, pride becomes a mask for pain.

Rather than admit we're hurt, we harden.

Rather than cry, we criticise.

Rather than admit we still care, we pretend we don't feel anything at all.

Michal may have seemed prideful, but her sarcasm was layered with sorrow.

Her contempt wasn't born in arrogance, it was born in abandonment.

Pride says:

"I don't need him."

"It doesn't hurt anymore."

"I'm over it."

But pain, if you listen closely, is whispering:

"I miss who we used to be."

"I wish I mattered to him the way I once did."

"I never got to say what it really did to me."

Many of us have built fortresses around our hearts, not because we are proud, but because we are tired of hurting in places we've never been healed.

- **The Silent Grief of Feeling Replaced**

Michal watched her husband bring the Ark home in public triumph, while her presence was irrelevant. Other women now occupied his heart and household. She had become a forgotten name in a story she helped start.

In modern relationships, this pain looks like:

Being sidelined by a partner's career, ministry, or ambition.

Watching someone you love move on without you, physically, emotionally, or spiritually.

Feeling stuck in the same place while they evolve into someone unrecognisable.

Realising they no longer see you and wondering if they ever truly did.

This kind of grief is complex because it's not always about a breakup.

Sometimes the relationship still exists, but the connection is gone.

You're still there, still loyal, still married or committed, but invisible. And invisibility hurts more than absence.

- **When You Love but Don't Feel Loved Back**

Michal's pain is the pain of many modern women who gave their hearts to someone who once cherished them, but now treats them like a relic of a past season.

The one who once saw your strength now treats you like an afterthought.

The one who praised your loyalty now criticises your emotions.

The one who once lit up at your presence now barely looks up.

Some of us have all fallen in love with a David before. A man with promise, passion, and power. But as life evolved, so did the distance between us. What began as romantic loyalty turned into emotional isolation. We loved this David for who he was, not who he has become. And when the version of that person we loved disappeared, our hearts never recovered. You fall in love with a man full of potential. A dreamer. A fighter. Someone who makes you feel chosen, seen, and inspired. But then life happens. The attention fades. The affection cools. Ambition changes him. Or maybe pain changes you. And yet, you're still holding on to the memory, not the man. You're in love with who he used to be, not who he is now. You stay, not because love is alive, but because grief hasn't been processed.

We often romanticise potential and get stuck in relationships that expired emotionally long ago. Like Michal, we end up at the window, watching someone we once loved worship freely, dance boldly, move forward, while we stand frozen, resenting the shift, yet too proud or too broken to release it. Michal's story teaches us: when the version you loved no longer exists, clinging to it will only deepen the pain. Freedom begins when you allow yourself to grieve the loss, bless the past, and let go.

Michal teaches us something vital:

You can't hold on to love and let go of yourself at the same time.

You can't live in the past and experience present joy.

You can't stay at the window and also dance in the presence of God.

A woman who keeps scrolling through old photos, hoping to find the version of him that used to hold her hand in public. Someone who remains legally or emotionally married to a person who has long checked out emotionally, but feels too ashamed to walk away. A once-hopeful romantic who now rolls her eyes at weddings and avoids joy because it feels like a betrayal of her pain. A woman deeply wounded by church, community, or family, watching from the sidelines but too hurt to reengage. +Michal's story warns us: when love becomes a prison, it's no longer love.

Letting Go of What No Longer Exists

There is no healing in holding on to ghosts.

You cannot keep replaying memories hoping they'll rewrite reality.

You cannot stay loyal to someone who exists only in your imagination.

God does not anoint you to chase shadows. He calls you into freedom.

Letting go does not mean it didn't matter.

Letting go does not mean it wasn't real.

Letting go simply means you are making room for what God wants to do next.

- **What do you do when the person you love becomes a stranger to your heart?**

Too often, like Michal, we respond not with vulnerability but with distance.

We build emotional walls to hide the ache. We let pride become our refuge because asking for connection feels too costly and too humiliating.

Michal's Missed Healing

Michal never got closure, not emotionally, not spiritually, not relationally.

And perhaps the most tragic part of her story is this: she never allowed herself to move past it.

She never learned to release what no longer served her.

She never opened her heart to the possibility of a new joy, a new identity, or a new purpose beyond David. And so, she remained frozen, resentful at the window, untouched by worship, unseen by the very man she once adored.

A Word for the Reader: Let the Tears Fall

You don't have to be "the strong one" all the time.

You don't have to cover your pain with sarcasm, pride, or coldness.

You're allowed to say, "That broke me."

You're allowed to miss someone who changed.

You're allowed to grieve what was and still open your hands to what will be.

The pain behind your pride doesn't disqualify you, it's where God wants to begin your healing

Modern Reflections of Michal

Reflection Questions

Are you in love with a memory or a present reality?

What relationship, title, or version of yourself have you refused to release, even though it no longer reflects who you are?

In what areas of your life are you watching from a window rather than engaging in joy?

Prayer for the Woman Still Looking Out the Window

God,
I confess that I have held on too long.
To people who left.
To dreams that died.
To versions of love that no longer serve me.
I've stood at the window long enough.
Today, I choose to step into Your presence, even with my bruises and questions.
Teach me to let go.
Heal me from what I can't fix.
Lead me from mourning into movement.
Amen.

Letting Go Moment

If you're holding on to a memory, a person, or a version of yourself that no longer exists, write a letter, not to send, but to release.

Start with:

"I loved you. But I'm letting you go now."

Write until you feel the weight lift, even just a little.

Then fold it, pray over it, and release it.

You don't need their permission to be free.

CHAPTER 5

Orpah — The Goodbye That Didn't Birth a Legacy

Theme: When turning back seems like the only option

Reflection: The cost of stopping short

Scripture Focus:

"Then Orpah kissed her mother-in-law goodbye, but Ruth clung to her."

Ruth 1:14 (NIV)

The Goodbye We Rarely Talk About

Orpah's name is mentioned only a few times. Her farewell is brief. Her path vanishes from the narrative. Yet within her quiet departure is a profound story, one that echoes the struggle of countless women. Orpah wasn't a villain.

She didn't abandon Naomi out of malice.

She had every logical reason to return home, her family, her culture, the familiarity of Moab.

Naomi herself encouraged it.

So, she wept, she kissed Naomi, and she walked away.

But while Ruth's clinging became the seed of legacy, Orpah's goodbye became the symbol of what could have been.

> *"The line between legacy and lost opportunity is often a single decision".*

When Going Back Feels Like the Only Way Forward

We all face moments when moving forward feels impossible.

When the road ahead is uncertain, and the past, though flawed, feels safer.

When faith asks us to step into unfamiliar territory without a guarantee.

When grief, fatigue, or fear weigh heavier than vision.

When we are convinced that we are not "the one" God will use.

Orpah chose the known over the unknown, she chose comfort over covenant. She chose predictability over possibility, and who can blame her?

The Cost of Stopping Short

Orpah walked far enough to feel the weight of the journey, but not far enough to see the reward.

She was on the road to Bethlehem, the house of bread, the place of provision, the land of legacy, but she stopped just before the breakthrough.

Many of us are walking that same line:

A woman pursuing her calling… until opposition whispers, "You're not equipped for this."

A single woman waiting for God's best… until loneliness tempts her to settle.

A dreamer with a God-given idea… until fear convinces her it's too late.

A woman healing from trauma… until the discomfort of growth makes going back seem easier.

How many times have we stopped short?

Not because we weren't called, but because the journey felt too costly.

Not because we didn't believe in God, but because we stopped believing He could still use us.

The Difference between Orpah and Ruth

Both Orpah and Ruth started in grief.

Both stood at the same crossroads.

Both had the chance to move forward into destiny.

But Ruth clung first to Naomi, then to God.

She chose covenant over comfort.

She risked everything and became part of the lineage of Christ.

Orpah's name disappears after her decision. Not because she was evil, but because she walked away from the unfolding of God's redemptive story.

> *"Sometimes legacy is born not through ability, but through persistence".*

Modern Reflections of Orpah

A young woman walks away from a ministry because it's too slow, too hard, too lonely.

A woman leaves her healing journey because reliving pain is uncomfortable.

A wife ends her marriage because restoration looked impossible, but didn't wait to see what God might still do.

A professional walks away from purpose to re-enter the rat race, because purpose takes longer to pay.

Like Orpah, many women weep sincerely, but still turn back.

They mean well. They love deeply. But fear or fatigue becomes the compass.

When It's Not Too Late to Turn Around

Here's the grace:

Even if you made an Orpah decision, God isn't finished with you.

Orpah's story may have ended in Scripture, but yours does not have to.

God is the Redeemer of detours, delays, and decisions made in weariness.

You can still say yes.

You can still cling.

You can still return to the journey and pick up where you left off.

"Legacy is not a matter of perfection, it's a matter of willingness".

Reflection Questions

Have you ever stopped short of something God was calling you into?

What have you walked away from, not out of rebellion, but out of fear or exhaustion?

Is there a place in your life where you need to cling again to purpose, to faith, to God?

Prayer for the One Who Turned Back

Father,

I admit there are moments when I gave up too soon.

Moments when I wept but still walked away.

I thank You for Your mercy that covers even my hesitations.

Today, I choose to return, not just in body, but in faith.

Give me the strength to finish what You started in me.

Let my story still echo legacy, even if I begin again.

Amen.

Letting Go Moment

Think of one "unfinished obedience" in your life, something you left behind because it was hard, scary, or unclear.

Write it down. Then write next to it:

"I'm not too late. God still writes stories with second chances."

CHAPTER 6

The Woman at the Well — Cycles That Never Let Go of You

Theme: Repeating patterns and emotional thirst

Reflection: What are you returning to for validation?

Scripture Focus:

"Everyone who drinks this water will be thirsty again, but whoever drinks the water I give them will never thirst."

John 4:13–14 (NIV)

The Woman No One Wanted to Talk To

She came to the well alone, at noon, in the heat of the day, when no one else dared to draw water.

Her shame had become her shadow.

This was the woman whose name we never learn, but whose story Jesus deliberately sought out. She had cycled through five husbands and was now with a man who wasn't her husband. Not only was her community avoiding her, she had learned to avoid them, too. But Jesus? He waited for her. He didn't meet her in a synagogue or a crowd. He met her in a dry place.

A quiet place.

A place of repetition.

A place where she returned daily, hoping for relief.

Not just physical thirst, but soul thirst.

The Repetition That Exhausts the Soul

Every day, she came to that well to draw water.

And yet every day, the water ran out.

He Met Her in a Dry Place

Not just physically dry, but emotionally barren.

She wasn't surrounded by friends or affirmation. She was alone.

She didn't come expecting a miracle, she came because routine demanded it.

But God doesn't always meet us in sanctuaries. Sometimes, He finds us in survival mode.

In the middle of nowhere. At noon. In the heat. When no one else is looking.

Sometimes, it's in your driest seasons, your emptiest, most repetitive, most disappointing seasons, that He shows up. A Quiet Place, there was no crowd, no fanfare, no applause. Just a woman trying to avoid shame and a

Saviour who made time for her story. God doesn't just speak in thunder, He meets us in the stillness, in the private, vulnerable moments when we've silenced everyone else.

This was a sacred interruption. He met her in the silence others avoided. Have you ever noticed how healing often begins where your noise ends?

A Place of Repetition

This wasn't her first visit to the well. She had done this day after day, hoping for relief and finding just enough to get by. **Draw, Carry, Return and Repeat.** She wasn't looking for transformation, she was just trying to survive the day. That's the weariness of spiritual repetition:

Doing what needs to be done, without knowing if it will ever truly fill the ache inside. Sometimes, the most desperate places are not dramatic, they're routine. A Place She Returned to Daily, hoping for relief. This well was more than a water source, it was the centre of her search. Every time she returned, she carried more than a jar, she carried the weight of disappointment, of loneliness of another night spent wondering why her story hadn't changed. Her body was thirsty, but so was her soul. She was tired of starting over, tired of giving and being left. Tired of feeling empty, even when her jar was full.

Not Just Physical Thirst, but Soul Thirst

She didn't know how to say it, but her soul was parched.

Not for more attention, but for affection that healed.

Not for another man, but for meaning that anchored her.

Not for one more chance, but for a fresh beginning that didn't require performance.

Jesus knew this wasn't just about water.

It was about a woman running on empty, emotionally, spiritually, relationally, and that's the thirst that many of us live with: The unspoken hunger for love, validation, purpose, and peace.

The Repetition that exhausts the Soul, and every day she came, every day she filled her jar.

And every day, it emptied again, that's what cycles do. They promise to quench, but they drain you instead. They look like relief, but they function like traps. You return to the well to the familiar pattern.

To the place that gives just enough to survive but never enough to thrive. It's the emotional treadmill: movement without progress. You go through the motions, but deep down, you're tired. Not just physically, but spiritually tired of being tired. And in that exhaustion, Jesus offers water that doesn't run dry.

Isn't that what cycles feel like?

You keep going back to the same place,

To the same relationships.

To the same habits.

To the same ways of coping.

To the same voices that don't affirm you but familiarise your wounds.

You keep hoping this time it'll fill you.

This time it'll satisfy. This time it'll be different, but it never is.

Because broken wells can't quench divine thirst.

The Wells We Keep Returning To

We may not all have five husbands, but we've all had patterns.

Places we keep revisiting in search of worth.

A toxic relationship that feels familiar even though it's not fulfilling.

Overworking to feel important because rest feels like failure.

Social media scrolling and comparisons that numb instead of nourish.

Giving too much in the hope that someone finally sees our value.

Spiritually dry seasons where performance replaces presence.

And like the woman at the well, we keep coming back.

Not because it works, but because it's what we know.

Sometimes bondage looks like routine.

When You Confuse Attachment for Healing

This woman wasn't just promiscuous, she was searching.

For safety.

For affection.

For belonging.

For a man to stay.

For a love that would finally prove she was worthy of being chosen and kept.

But the tragedy of emotional thirst is this: It can drive you into the arms of people who only deepen your ache.

And she thought she needed another relationship. Jesus offered her revelation.

She wanted validation - He offered her truth.

She expected judgment - He gave her transformation.

Attachment vs. Healing: What Are You Clinging To?

The Woman at the Well wasn't just moving from one man to the next, she was clinging to hope that someone, somewhere, would make her feel whole. But broken attachment doesn't lead to healing. It creates cycles that feel like love but are actually patterns of self-preservation and fear.

Understanding Attachment Styles

Our patterns of connection, how we bond, seek closeness, and handle rejection, are often rooted in attachment styles formed early in life but replayed in our adult relationships. Let's briefly explore them:

1. Anxious Attachment

You crave closeness, but fear abandonment.

You may become clingy, overly accommodating, or emotionally dependent.

You may find yourself constantly wondering: "Do they really love me?" "Did I do something wrong?"

In the woman at the well: Her history suggests she might have latched on to relationships out of fear of being alone, seeking safety in men, even if the love was inconsistent.

Modern example:

A woman stays in a relationship that doesn't serve her but because the thought of starting over feels more painful than being mistreated. She overextends, apologises excessively, and feels anxious when her partner pulls away.

2. Avoidant Attachment

You value independence over intimacy.

You may push people away when they get too close or when emotions feel overwhelming.

You tend to hide feelings to avoid vulnerability.

In the woman at the well: After five failed relationships, she may have grown numb. Detached. Protecting her heart by keeping connections superficial, transactional, probably with the sixth man.

Modern example:

A woman constantly changes partners, avoids deep commitment, or shuts down emotionally in conflict, mistaking detachment for strength.

3. Fearful-Avoidant (Disorganised) Attachment

You want love but fear it at the same time.

You may have a history of trauma, rejection, or abandonment.

You send mixed signals: come close, then push away.

In the woman at the well: There's no stability in her relationships, only survival. She may be caught in a loop of longing and fleeing. Wanting to be known, but fearing the cost of being seen.

Modern example:

A woman desires connection but sabotages intimacy. She may have trust issues, cycles of toxic love, and a deep fear that everyone eventually leaves.

4. Secure Attachment

You feel safe giving and receiving love.

You're emotionally available, but not emotionally dependent.

You can set boundaries, communicate openly, and maintain a strong sense of self.

What Jesus offered the woman at the well:

A relationship rooted not in neediness or power, but in identity, safety, and truth.

He didn't use her. He didn't shame her. He saw her and stayed.

That's what secure attachment with God creates: Wholeness without performance, love without fear and belonging that isn't earned, but given

In Our Era: How Broken Attachment Shows Up

In today's world, many of us women struggle with hidden attachment wounds that influence our choices:

Social media validation: Constantly posting or seeking attention to feel visible or desirable.

Serial dating or hook-ups: Confusing physical touch with emotional connection.

Over functioning in relationships: Doing more than your share, to "earn" love.

Avoiding intimacy altogether: Claiming independence while secretly fearing vulnerability.

Staying stuck in cycles: Going back to toxic exes, repeating family patterns, or staying too long in the name of "loyalty." We mask it with busyness, with spirituality, with perfectionism, with overachievement, but deep down, we're thirsty for something only healing can give.

From Attachment to Healing: What Jesus Teaches Us

When Jesus encountered the woman at the well, He wasn't just offering her insight. He was offering her identity.

He didn't say, "You need another man."

He said, "You need living water."

You need something that doesn't break, disappoint, or leave.

He was essentially saying:

"You're looking for wholeness in places that can't hold you. Let me be the well you stop thirsting at."

Healing begins when You stop outsourcing your worth, you recognise your patterns for what they are.

When you let God touch the root, not just the behaviour, you allow yourself to be loved without needing to earn it. Because Jesus Doesn't Shame, He Satisfies

When Jesus met this woman, He didn't condemn her.

He didn't list her failures, and he didn't tell her to clean up first.

He simply told her the truth about her patterns… and then offered her a better way.

"If you drink this water, you'll thirst again."

"But if you drink from Me, you'll never thirst again."

This wasn't just about water, it was about the source of her identity. Jesus offered her the thing every soul craves: To be seen. To be known. To be loved anyway. When You Walk Away from the Old Well

One of the most powerful moments in the story is this:

"Then, leaving her water jar, the woman went back to the town…" (John 4:28)

She left her jar. The very thing she had carried every day, the thing she thought she needed, she dropped it. Because when you encounter real healing, you no longer need the containers you used to cope. She ran back to the same people who once shamed her, not to defend herself, but to declare:

"Come, see a man who told me everything I ever did!"

She had moved from secrecy to testimony. From thirst to overflow, from cycle to calling.

Modern Reflections of the Woman at the Well

A woman who goes from man to man, hoping each one will heal what the last one broke.

A people-pleaser whose identity is tethered to being needed, even at the expense of her soul.

A woman who has never stopped to ask, "Why do I keep choosing this?"

A believer who knows the church but has never felt whole.

A high-achiever masking spiritual emptiness with productivity.

This story isn't just about one woman.

It's about any of us who confuse motion with meaning.

Any of us who are tired of thirsting but don't know how to stop drinking from the wrong source.

Reflection Questions

What "well" do you keep returning to that never truly satisfies?

Are there patterns in your life you've normalised but haven't questioned?

What would it look like to "leave your jar" and walk in healing?

What is your attachment style, and how has it shaped your relationships or spiritual life?

Who or what have you been clinging to for emotional survival rather than healing?

What would it look like for you to detach from the cycle and root yourself in God's love instead?

Prayer for the Thirsty Soul

Jesus,

You see my cycles.

You see the places I keep returning to, out of habit, out of hurt, out of fear.

And yet you still wait for me.

You offer water that satisfies.

Not temporary comfort, but lasting identity.

Teach me to stop striving and start surrendering.

I don't just want to be filled, I want to be changed.

Amen.

Letting Go Moment

On a blank page, write:

"I've been returning for worth, but it has never satisfied me."

Then write underneath it:

"Today, I lay down my jar and receive living water."

Let this become the moment you trade repetition for revelation.

Enjoy the words in this Song

Fill My Cup, Lord

Like the woman at the well
I was seeking
For things that could not satisfy
And then I heard my Savior speaking
"Draw from My well that never shall run dry"
Fill my cup, Lord
I lift it up, Lord
Come and quench this thirsting of my soul
Bread of Heaven, feed me 'til I want no more
Fill my cup, fill it up and make me whole
There are millions in this world
Who are craving
The pleasures, earthly things of gold
But none can match the wondrous treasure
That I find in Jesus Christ my Lord
Fill my cup, Lord
I lift it up, Lord
Come and quench this thirsting of my soul
Bread of Heaven, feed me 'til I want no more
Fill my cup, fill it up and make me whole
Here's my cup, fill it up and make me whole

CHAPTER 7

Sapphira — When Letting Go Means Letting Go of Control

Theme: Hidden motives, deceit, and fear of transparency

Reflection: The control we don't want to surrender to God

Scripture Focus:

"About three hours later, his wife came in, not knowing what had happened. Peter asked her, 'Tell me, is this the price you and Ananias got for the land?' 'Yes,' she said, 'that is the price.' Peter said to her, 'How could you conspire to test the Spirit of the Lord?'"

Acts 5:7–9 (NIV)

The Woman Who Didn't Want to Let Go Completely

Sapphira and her husband, Ananias, had the appearance of generosity.

They sold a piece of land, like many others in the early church, and brought the money to the apostles. But unlike others, they secretly held back part of the proceeds while pretending to give it all.

There was no requirement to give everything, but they wanted the recognition without the sacrifice.

They wanted to appear surrendered without actually surrendering.

Control hid behind their generosity.

Pride cloaked itself as piety.

And Sapphira followed along, knowing, agreeing, and protecting the lie.

When Appearances Matter More Than Authenticity

Sapphira wasn't just part of the plan, she was complicit in the performance.

She knew the truth but chose the image.

She held back the money, but more dangerously, she held back the truth.

In our world, Sapphira's story plays out often:

The woman who wears spiritual language to cover emotional distance from God.

The perfectionist who appears faithful but is silently driven by fear.

The believer who tithes, serves, or leads, but still withholds obedience in private matters.

The couple who posts unity on social media but live in silence and secrets at home.

The desire to look surrendered without truly being surrendered is a subtle form of control.

Control: The Idol We Don't Want to Name

Sapphira's greatest struggle wasn't money. It was control.

Control of how she was perceived.

Control over how much she would let go.

Control over the narrative and outcome.

Control over her image rather than her intimacy with God.

Control often disguises itself as responsibility, strength, or wisdom. But at its root, it's a refusal to trust.

We control when we don't believe God will come through.

We control when we fear being exposed.

We control because surrender feels like a risk, and our survival instincts have been trained to avoid vulnerability at all costs.

The Cost of Hidden Motives:

What made Sapphira's story tragic wasn't just the act, it was the motive behind it.

She and Ananias weren't punished for what they gave, but for pretending to be something they weren't. They wanted the reward without the reality, the applause without the alignment.

The platform without the purity. God doesn't demand perfection, He desires honesty.

But Sapphira chose secrecy, and secrecy, when wrapped in pride, becomes deadly to the soul.

Modern Reflections of Sapphira

A woman who agrees with things in a relationship she knows aren't right because she fears conflict or rejection.

A ministry leader who smiles in public but harbours bitterness, addiction, or unconfessed compromise.

A Christian who gives a portion of their heart to God, but not their pain, their finances, their past, or their future.

A woman who says "God, use me," but with strings attached: "As long as I'm still in control. As long as it doesn't cost too much. As long as I look good doing it."

Sapphira's story reminds us:

God isn't after your image. He's after your heart.

The Fear of Full Transparency

Why didn't Sapphira confess when Peter asked her directly?

Because fear still had a grip.

Fear of exposure.

Fear of the consequences.

Fear of admitting she wasn't as "together" as she appeared.

But healing doesn't come through performance.

Breakthrough doesn't come through appearances.

Freedom comes through truth. Even painful truth.

> *"Sometimes, what's killing us isn't what we did but it's what we refuse to admit we're still holding on to".*

What Are You Still Controlling?

Ask yourself:

What part of my life have I labelled as "surrendered" but still secretly control?

What image do I protect more than my intimacy with God?

What truths am I scared to speak out loud, even in prayer?

Letting go of control doesn't make you weak.

It makes you available for real transformation.

Because what you release, God can redeem.

But what you hide, you give the enemy permission to manipulate.

Reflection Questions

Where in your life are you more concerned with appearing surrendered than being surrendered?

What area of your life have you partially given to God, but not fully?

Are there secrets or compromises that feel "small" but are quietly hardening your heart?

Prayer for the Woman Holding the Reins

God,
I confess that I like to be in control.
I want safety. I want certainty. I want to protect my image.
But You are not fooled by my performances.
You see the hidden places, and You love me still.
Give me the courage to surrender fully.
To tell the truth. To lay it all down.
I don't want to live a lie.
I want to live in freedom.
Amen.

Letting Go Moment

Write down the things you still try to control, your image, your relationships, your finances, your future.

Then write across them:

"God, I release this. I surrender what I can't control to the One who can."

Say it out loud. Pray it from your heart.

And choose to walk away from the need to "seem" surrendered, and into the freedom of actually being surrendered.

CHAPTER 8

Herodias's Daughter — When Vengeance Becomes Your Vision

Theme: Holding onto generational offence and bitterness

Reflection: Are you dancing for someone else's grudge?

Scripture Focus:

"Prompted by her mother, she said, 'Give me here on a platter the head of John the Baptist.'"

Matthew 14:8 (NIV)

Two Women, One Dangerous Dance

The daughter of Herodias is nameless in Scripture, but her moment is unforgettable.

She dances before King Herod and his guests, pleasing them so much that he offers her anything she wants, up to half his kingdom. But instead of choosing a crown, a treasure, or her own destiny, she turns to her mother. And Herodias whispers her long-nurtured grudge into her daughter's ear.

"Ask for the head of John the Baptist."

And so the girl returns with the request not from her own heart, but from her mother's hatred.

A young woman's influence is used not for healing, but for vengeance. The Silent Weight of Inherited Wounds, this is not just a story about a murder. It's a story about how bitterness spreads. Herodias hated John the Baptist because he called out her unlawful marriage to Herod. Her offence became an obsession. She waited for the right moment and when it came, she used her daughter to execute it.

The daughter had no quarrel with John, she wasn't even part of the original offence. But she became a carrier of her mother's pain. How often does this happen in our own lives?

A daughter who grows up hating a relative she never knew, because her mother never healed.

A woman who mistrusts men because the women before her were betrayed.

A friend who withdraws from the community because her mentor modelled bitterness as strength.

A believer who distances herself from the church because someone else's unresolved offence became her narrative.

You don't have to be the one who was wounded to live wounded. Sometimes bitterness is inherited, quietly, gradually, and generationally.

When Someone Else's Grudge Becomes Your Purpose

Herodias's daughter wasn't just manipulated, she was misguided. Her moment of influence was poisoned by unresolved bitterness. Instead of asking, "What do I want"? She asked, "What do you want me to do?"

That's the tragedy of many of us women today:

Living our lives to prove someone else wrong.

Making decisions not out of purpose but out of pain that isn't even ours. Using our gifts to please, to avenge, to protect someone else's ego, rather than walk in their God-given call. You were never meant to dance for someone else's grudge.

The Limitations of Carrying Someone Else's Bitterness

Bitterness is heavy on its own.

But when the weight isn't even yours, it becomes soul-crushing.

Carrying someone else's resentment may feel like loyalty.

It may be dressed up as support, protection, or even righteousness.

But ultimately, it's a trap, because bitterness borrowed still binds you.

1. It Distorts Your Identity

When you carry unresolved anger that isn't yours:

You begin to mirror someone else's wounds, not your true self.

You lose clarity about your own convictions.

You confuse your own story with someone else's trauma.

Like Herodias's daughter, you may begin to speak and act from second-hand offence, eventually living out a script that was never meant for you.

You can't become who God called you to be if you're still performing someone else's pain.

2. It Limits Your Voice

Bitterness has a way of silencing you, especially when it's inherited.

You may feel torn between honouring someone's hurt and standing in truth.

But the moment you begin to shape your responses around their offence, your voice no longer sounds like your own.

You might withhold grace because they couldn't forgive.

You might avoid reconciliation because they burned the bridge.

You might become sceptical, guarded, or harsh, not because of your own experience, but theirs.

When your voice becomes an echo of someone else's resentment, you lose the power of your own testimony.

3. It Delays Your Healing

Healing requires honesty.

But if you're carrying someone else's bitterness, you may be treating wounds you don't actually have, and neglecting the ones you do.

Bitterness by proxy:

Can mask your real needs.

Can create false battles and misplaced priorities.

Can entangle you in emotional wars that have nothing to do with your calling.

You cannot heal what you don't own.

And you can't fully walk in freedom if part of your emotional landscape still belongs to someone else's storm.

4. It Compromises Your Discernment

When your heart is clouded with borrowed bitterness:

You struggle to see people clearly.

You second-guess good things because someone else once told you, "They're all like that."

You sabotage opportunities out of fear inherited from others' experiences.

Just like Herodias's daughter didn't stop to discern truth for herself, many today are caught in decisions based not on revelation, but relational manipulation.

Resentment distorts discernment.

And when your lens is cloudy, your decisions will always be misaligned.

5. It Blocks Legacy and Purpose

What if Herodias's daughter had chosen differently?

What if she had asked, "Why does my mother want this?"

What if she had sought God's voice instead of Herodias's anger?

Her story could've been one of healing, a woman who broke a generational curse of revenge.

Instead, her legacy was sealed in blood for a wound that wasn't hers.

Likewise, the longer you carry someone else's bitterness:

The more you miss your own assignments.

The more your gifts are redirected toward protecting someone else's pain instead of healing your own community. The more you trade your divine legacy for borrowed battles. Bitterness may be inherited, but legacy must be chosen.

Let's understand that loyalty shouldn't cost you your soul

You can love someone deeply and still refuse to carry their unhealed pain.

You can honour their story without living it out.

You can choose truth over alliance, peace over performance, and freedom over familiarity.

When you release what was never yours to carry, you give God permission to rewrite your future—clean of inherited rage and full of redemptive purpose.

The Power of Unhealed Matriarchs

Herodias is a cautionary figure not because she was angry, but because she never dealt with the root of that anger. She was powerful, she was persuasive, but she was poisoned. When a mother, mentor, or matriarch harbours bitterness, her influence becomes a filter. Her voice shapes the next generation, not with wisdom, but with resentment. And the daughters, unless discerning, begin to carry burdens that don't belong to them.

We must ask:

Are we repeating cycles we never chose?

Are we angry at people who never hurt us?

Are we living small because someone else modelled unforgiveness as loyalty?

Modern Reflections of Herodias's Daughter

A woman who sabotages healthy relationships because someone taught her that love is dangerous.

A daughter who distrusts leadership because of her mother's offence against authority.

A friend who cuts off people based on someone else's pain, not her own discernment.

A believer who walks away from destiny to protect a toxic alliance.

Sometimes we say it's "support", but really, we're just echoing someone else's unhealed past.

Healing the Bitterness You Didn't Start

If Herodias's daughter had paused long enough to ask God, "What do you want for me?"

Her legacy might have been different.

But she danced for applause.

She danced for a manipulator.

And she danced away from her own freedom.

Let this chapter remind you: you are allowed to put down what was never yours.

You are not called to continue cycles of silent revenge. You are not obligated to inherit anyone's hatred. You can break the chain by choosing healing over loyalty to pain.

Reflection Questions

Are there areas in your life where you are reacting to pain that didn't start with you?

Have you ever followed someone's offence out of loyalty, rather than truth?

What generational emotions, bitterness, distrust, anger, do you need to release so you can be free?

Prayer for the One Carrying Someone Else's Grief

Lord,

Show me the places where I've inherited pain I was never meant to carry.

Reveal the grudges I'm holding that aren't mine.

Heal the wounds I adopted through loyalty, silence, or fear.

Give me the courage to choose purpose over bitterness.

Let me dance only for your glory not for applause, not for revenge, not for borrowed pain.

Amen.

Here are some songs to reflect on

🎵 1. "Let There Be Peace on Earth" (Traditional Hymn)

Key lyrics:

"Let peace begin with me, let this be the moment now…"

This hymn emphasizes breaking the cycle and choosing peace, even when past generations have chosen otherwise. It aligns well with the decision not to carry inherited bitterness forward.

🎵 2. "Break Every Chain", Jesus Culture / Tasha Cobbs

Key lyrics:

"There is power in the name of Jesus to break every chain…"

This anthem speaks directly to generational bondage. If the daughter in the story had turned to Christ instead of following her mother's grudge, the chains could have broken. This song is a bold declaration of choosing deliverance over a destructive legacy.

🎵 3. "I Surrender", Hillsong Worship

Key lyrics:

"I surrender all to You / Everything I give to You…"

A deep cry of surrender, this song fits the chapter's invitation to release control, bitterness, and emotional entanglement passed down from others. It's a modern-day response to inherited pain.

🎵 4. "Clean", Natalie Grant

Key lyrics:

"There's nothing too dirty / That You can't make worthy…"

This powerful ballad speaks to those who have lived in the aftermath of others' choices. It's for the woman who wants to be free from the stain of someone else's offence. It brings a redemptive close to the heaviness of bitterness.

🎵 5. "Generations", Sarah Kroger

Key lyrics:

"Let every generation know / You are faithful…"

This beautiful song is a prophetic declaration of breaking cycles and allowing God's love and truth to rewrite family legacy. It contrasts with the story of Herodias by offering a vision of generational healing.

Letting Go Moment

Write down one belief, emotion, or relational pattern that was passed down to you, intentionally or not, that no longer serves your healing.

Then write:

"This ends with me. I release what was never mine to carry."

Let that become a generational turning point.

Optional Reflection Activity

Play "Break Every Chain" or "I Surrender."

As the music plays, reflect on this prompt:

"Whose emotional burden have I carried too long? What would it feel like to lay it down?"

Then write:

"This is the moment I choose peace over bitterness, truth over loyalty to pain, and healing over generational hurt."

CONCLUSION

The Woman Who Let Go

Letting go brings healing, purpose, and redemption

Reflection: What might your life look like if you truly let go?

She Came in with Her Past but Left with Her Purpose

She wasn't invited.

She had no place at the table.

She was known in the city not for her reputation of virtue, but for her brokenness.

And yet... she came. Carrying an alabaster jar, costly, precious, and symbolic of everything she had this unnamed woman in Luke 7 stood at the feet of Jesus.

She broke open her offering.

She wept without shame.

She poured out her past.

And she walked away in peace.

She didn't explain.

She didn't justify.

She just… let go.

The Courage to Let Go

Unlike Lot's wife, she didn't look back.

Unlike Sapphira, she didn't pretend.

Unlike Herodias, she didn't plot.

Unlike Orpah, she didn't turn back before the blessing.

This woman pushed past shame.

She broke protocol.

She risked exposure.

And in doing so, she received what so many others never did: freedom.

Jesus said of her, *"Her many sins have been forgiven—as her great love has shown."* (Luke 7:47)

Letting go is love in motion.

Love for the God who restores.

Love yourself enough to walk out of the prison of your past and into the promise of your future.

Mary Magdalene: From Possession to Purpose

Then there's Mary Magdalene.

Once tormented by seven demons, bound, broken, and forgotten.

Until she met Jesus, she didn't just let go of darkness and follow the Light.

She became one of His most faithful disciples.

She stood at the cross when others fled.

She went to the tomb when others gave up.

And she was the first to witness the resurrected Christ.

From possessed to proclaimer, her healing became her mission. When you let go of the past, God gives you a future worth living for.

You Are Not Herodias's Daughter.

You don't have to dance for someone else's pain.

You don't have to perform for approval.

You don't have to hide behind survival.

You don't have to pretend you're over it when you're not.

You don't have to stay frozen in the past.

You can be the woman who lets go.

The woman who broke the jar.

The woman who poured it out.

The woman who followed Jesus without turning back.

The woman who said, "Yes" to healing, even if it cost her comfort.

You can be the woman who interrupts a generational cycle.

Who released control.

Who turned grief into grace.

Who walked out of bitterness and into peace.

You can be the woman who surrendered and stepped into destiny.

Reflection Questions

What have you been afraid to release because it gave you identity, comfort, or control?

Who do you become when you stop performing and start pouring at the feet of Jesus?

Are you ready to become the woman who lets go?

Final Prayer: For the Woman Becoming Free

Jesus,

I've seen what happens when women stay frozen.

When bitterness, shame, pride, and fear become prisons.

But I want more.

I want freedom.

I want healing.

I want to walk in purpose.

I don't want to live defined by what hurt me.

I want to be remembered as the woman who let go, and lived.

Amen.

Letting Go Moment

Write this in your journal:

"Today I stop surviving the past and start stepping into my purpose. I am not frozen. I am free."

Sign it. Date it. Declare it.

The Woman Who Reached

Letting go of shame and isolation to touch what heals

Reflection: What would change in your life if you stopped hiding and reached out in faith?

Twelve Years Is a Long Time to Bleed

She had been bleeding for twelve years.

Not just physically, but emotionally.

Twelve years of being labelled "unclean."

Twelve years of doctor visits, empty promises, and depleted savings.

Twelve years of being isolated, avoided, and excluded from community, affection, and worship.

Twelve years of silent suffering.

And yet, she kept her faith alive.

She had every reason to give up.

Every reason to believe healing wasn't possible.

But instead of staying hidden, she did something radical.

She let go of fear… and reached.

She Reached Through the Shame

She didn't make an announcement.

She didn't ask for permission.

She didn't even try to get Jesus' full attention.

She simply believed:

"If I can just touch the hem of His garment…" That tiny thread of hope was enough.

And when her fingers brushed the edge of His robe, everything changed.

Instantly, the bleeding stopped.

Instantly, she felt whole.

Instantly, Jesus noticed.

> *"Who touched Me?" He asked, not to shame her, but to acknowledge her.*

Because faith that reaches even in secret always gets Heaven's attention.

Letting go of Fear to Walk in Wholeness, this woman didn't just let go of blood…

She let go of:

Fear of rejection

Shame about her condition

Exhaustion from years of disappointment

The lie that her healing wasn't worth pursuing, she chose to believe that touching Jesus, even quietly, was enough. And she was right.

> *"Daughter, your faith has made you well. Go in peace." (Luke 8:48)*

Jesus called her Daughter.

Not outcast.

Not problem.

Not unclean.

Daughter.

She let go of twelve years of silence and grabbed hold of one moment with the Saviour, and it changed everything.

You Can Reach Too

Maybe you've been bleeding emotionally, privately, quietly. Maybe you've gotten good at hiding your pain. Maybe you've tried everything and nothing's worked. But one touch of faith can still change everything. This isn't about dramatics, this is about desperate, focused, surrendered faith, the kind that says, *"I refuse to live like this anymore. I'm reaching for healing."* You don't need to be seen by a crowd, you just need to touch Jesus.

Reflection Questions

What have you been carrying for too long that needs to be released at His feet?

What lie has convinced you that healing is for everyone else, but not you?

Are you ready to reach, no matter what people say, think, or assume?

Prayer for the Woman Who's Ready to Reach

Jesus,
I've tried everything else.
I've hidden my pain for too long.
But today, I'm reaching for you.
Not for approval, not for applause, just for healing.
I believe one touch is all it takes.
Call me "Daughter." Make me whole.
Amen.

Letting Go Moment

Close your eyes. Picture the hem of His robe in front of you.

Whisper this aloud:

"I let go of shame, and I reach for healing. I am not invisible. I am not forgotten. I am whole."

Final Reflection: The Woman Who Reached

She wasn't frozen.

She was bleeding. Quietly. Constantly. Painfully.

For twelve long years, she carried what no one could see, disappointment, shame, and isolation.

Doctors couldn't help. People avoided her.

But still… she hoped.

And when Jesus passed by, she did something many never dared to do:

She reached. She Didn't reach loudly, she Reached Boldly

This was not a performance. She didn't ask for attention or applause.

She reached for the edge of His garment because she believed even that would be enough.

"If I can just touch Him…" (Mark 5:28)

She let go of:

Fear of rejection

Her identity as "the unclean one"

The opinions of the crowd

The need for full understanding

And in return, she received something far more powerful than healing: identity.

"Daughter, your faith has made you well." (Mark 5:34)

What She Teaches Us

While many of the women in this book show us what it looks like to hold on to pain, pride, or the past, this woman shows us what it looks like to press through it.

She didn't have the strength to fight, so she reached in faith.

She didn't demand a spotlight, she simply touched what she believed could save her.

She didn't stay in the crowd of stories marked by bitterness.

She wrote a new one, marked by boldness, belief, and breakthrough.

You Can Reach Too

Maybe you've been quietly bleeding.

Maybe no one knows how much you've endured.

Maybe shame has kept you in hiding.

But today, like her, you get to decide:

"I'm not staying in this condition."

"I'm not carrying this forever."

"I'm reaching, even if I have to crawl to Him."

And when you do, He'll meet you with compassion, not condemnation.

He won't just stop your bleeding.

He'll call you "Daughter."

He'll speak peace over your storm.

He'll send you forward, whole.

Reflection Questions

What have you been quietly bleeding from that needs the healing touch of Jesus?

What fears or opinions have kept you from reaching for more?

What would change in your life if you reached out in faith, even if no one else understood?

Letting Go Moment

Close your eyes and visualise Jesus walking by.

See yourself crawling past shame, labels, and fear.

Stretch out your hand and whisper:

"I let go of silence. I let go of shame. I reach for healing, and I receive it."

Write this in your journal:

"Like the woman who reached, I will not stay where pain has left me. I am whole."

EPILOGUE

A Letter to the Woman Becoming Free

Dear Woman, Wife, Mother, Aunty, Sister and Daughter of Courage,

If you've made it to this page, then I know something about you:

You didn't just read, you reflected.

You didn't just observe the stories of these women, you saw glimpses of yourself.

In their fears.

In their silence.

In their decisions.

In their desire to hold on… and maybe now, in your readiness to let go.

You've walked through the frozen places, places where grief, pride, shame, or disappointment kept women stuck.

But you also encountered those who reached, who surrendered, who chose healing even when it cost them everything.

And now, it's your turn.

Letting Go Is Not an Ending, It's an Opening

Letting go is not about forgetting.

It's not pretending that the pain didn't happen.

It's about refusing to live stuck in it.

It's about no longer giving the past permission to define you.

You may still be healing.

You may still be navigating unanswered questions.

But you've already made the most powerful move:

You chose to keep walking forward.

This Is Your Legacy Now

You are no longer the woman frozen in what was.

You are the woman reaching for what can be.

You are the woman who doesn't need to perform for love.

Who no longer dances for someone else's grudge.

Who doesn't pretend to be whole, because you are becoming whole, boldly and beautifully.

You are the woman who reaches for Jesus.

Who pours out what's costly.

Who breaks jars, touches robes, and walks away in peace.

You are not like Lot's wife.

You are not bound like Herodias.

You are not silenced like Sapphira.

You are the woman who let go.

And now… your story gets to be rewritten.

My Final Prayer for You

May you never again settle in places God is calling you out of.

May you release what you were never meant to carry.

May you forgive, even when there's no apology.

May you reach, even when you feel like hiding.

May you choose wholeness over bitterness, surrender over control, and purpose over pride.

May your future be proof that healing is real,

That God is faithful,

And that is the most powerful story…

Is the one where you didn't look back.

With love and belief in your becoming,

   — **Rebecca Obeng**

GLOSSARY

Alabaster Jar

A precious, sealed container often filled with expensive perfume or oil. In Scripture, it symbolises sacrifice, worship, and the releasing of something valuable to honour God. Breaking the jar represents total surrender.

Attachment (Emotional/Relational)

A deep emotional bond is formed in relationships, often shaped by early experiences. Unhealthy attachment can lead to fear of abandonment, over-dependence, or staying in toxic situations. Healing involves learning to anchor identity and worth in God.

Bitterness

A deep-seated resentment that poisons the soul and limits growth. It often stems from unresolved pain or injustice. Bitterness is a recurring theme in this book as a force that keeps people emotionally frozen.

Breakthrough

A spiritual and emotional turning point where healing, clarity, or freedom is experienced. Often comes after surrender, truth-telling, or divine intervention.

Control (Spiritual/Emotional)

The attempt to manage outcomes, emotions, or people out of fear or pride. Letting go of control is a recurring theme, surrendering to God's will is essential for healing and peace.

Cycles (Emotional or Generational)

Patterns of behaviour, dysfunction, or trauma that repeat across seasons or generations. Breaking cycles often requires intentional healing, new choices, and spiritual intervention.

Daughter

More than a biological identity, this term in the book symbolises belonging, restoration, and divine affirmation, mainly when used by Jesus to address the woman with the issue of blood.

Frozen

Used metaphorically to describe emotional paralysis or being stuck in the past, whether through pain, unforgiveness, or fear. A woman who is frozen cannot fully step into her purpose until she begins to thaw through truth and surrender.

Generational Pain

Emotional wounds, beliefs, or behaviours passed down from one generation to the next. It can be inherited through silence, bitterness, or modelled dysfunction.

Grudge

Persistent resentment toward someone who has caused harm. When passed from one person to another, especially across generations, it creates emotional bondage.

Healing (Emotional/Spiritual)

A process of restoration from emotional wounds, trauma, or spiritual disconnection. Often includes honesty, forgiveness, surrender, and the love of God.

Letting Go

The act of releasing control, shame, offence, or anything that keeps a person stuck. It is a foundational theme in the book and often marks the beginning of transformation.

Reaching

Used symbolically to describe an act of faith, as seen in the woman with the issue of blood. It represents pursuit, hope, and desperate belief in God's healing power.

Redemption

God's ability to restore, rebuild, and repurpose what was once broken, sinful, or lost. It's the promise that no past is beyond His power to make new.

Resentment

Unresolved anger or disappointment is often hidden under surface emotions. Resentment can quietly control behaviour and decision-making.

Surrender

Yielding control, outcomes, or emotions to God in trust. True surrender is not weakness but the gateway to peace, purpose, and divine alignment.

Transparency

The act of being open, honest, and vulnerable, especially with God. Transparency breaks the power of secrecy and begins the process of healing.

ACKNOWLEDGMENTS

Writing this book was not just a project, it was a process of healing, remembering, and releasing. It called me to revisit difficult places and let go of burdens I didn't know I was still carrying. To all who stood by me through this journey, thank you.

To God, my source, healer, and redeemer, thank You for showing me that even when we are frozen, You are not. You move. You reach. You restore. Thank you for calling me to write about women who couldn't let go, so I could become the woman who finally did.

To every woman whose story is found in these pages, whether in the Bible or in the world around me, thank you for living boldly, honestly, or brokenly. Your lives echo lessons we still need today.

To my family and friends, thank you for giving me grace when I needed silence, for cheering me on when I doubted, and for believing in the voice God placed within me. Your encouragement was the warmth I needed to thaw out the fear.

To my readers, thank you for saying "yes" to this journey. I don't take lightly the weight of the stories you carry. My prayer is that these pages lead you to your own "letting go" moment and that you walk away freer, lighter, and full of holy expectation for what comes next.

To those who walked with me in seasons of pain, delay, or discouragement, your impact helped shape these chapters. You may never know how much your words, prayers, or quiet presence meant.

To my editor, creative partners, and spiritual mentors, thank you for stewarding this message with care, precision, and spiritual insight. You sharpened what was raw, honoured what was sacred, and made the message clearer than I could have alone.

This book is for every woman who's been frozen.

May you melt in the warmth of grace.

May you reach like the woman who bled.

And may you rise like the woman who let go.

With love and deep gratitude,

Rebecca Obeng

READER NOTES

Take a quiet moment to reflect. These pages are just for you. your thoughts, your journey, your growth.

What stood out to you most in this book?

_____
_____
_____
_____
_____
_____

How has your perspective shifted or deepened?

_____
_____
_____
_____
_____
_____

Is there something God revealed to you while reading?

_____
_____
_____
_____
_____
_____

What's one step you will take after reading this?

_____
_____
_____
_____
_____
_____

Open Lined Notes Page

Your Quiet Space

Use this page for your prayers, thoughts, or any notes you'd like to keep close.

_____
_____
_____
_____
_____
_____
_____
_____
_____
_____
_____
_____
_____
_____
_____
_____
_____
_____
_____
_____
_____
_____

www.ingramcontent.com/pod-product-compliance
Lightning Source LLC
Chambersburg PA
CBHW070458090426
42735CB00012B/2605